FINGERPRINTS OF GOD

TAKING A CLOSER LOOK

Also available from the author:

Rearview Sunset – A Novel (2009)

FINGERPRINTS OF GOD

TAKING A CLOSER LOOK

BRETT CHAMPAN

NorthWaters
PRESS

Published by NorthWaters Press, Wisconsin
Style Edited by D. Michael
Copy Edited by W. Huska
Formatted and Printed by Publishers ExpressPress, Ladysmith, WI
Cover design by Karin Henley Designs

ISBN: 978-1-935920-03-8

Printed in the United States of America

Contents

To family dwelling in the city,
woods, and lands beyond the sea,
and to the Maker of fire and water
who seals us with an eternal destiny,

Thank you for your fingerprints in my life.

Thirsty hearts are those whose longings have been wakened by the touch of God within them.

A.W. Tozer

Introduction

An Invitation to Go Deeper

"I Am Who I Am." The words spoken by God to Moses long ago kept coming back to me. I could hear them in the recesses of my mind each time I sat down in my little cabin in the woods, where I was preparing a series of messages for a youth group retreat in the bush of Ontario, Canada.

When the week in the wilderness arrived, these words came even more alive.

"I Am Who I Am."

God is big, powerful. To look at a great mountain or ponder the power of rivers, seas, and storms provides evidence of this. He is everywhere all the time; there is no place where he cannot see and hear. He knows all things, even the deepest places of our souls. He is uncreated. He transcends definition. Even wisdom submits to him. Omnipotent, omnipresent, and omniscient. He is beyond.

Although God is beyond, he reveals himself in many ways. His *fingerprints* are all around us. They are on the campfires we so enjoy sitting around, in the majestic rivers that flow into the sea, in the wind that moves through the trees above, in the storms and rainbows that stir our senses, and in the stars that bring light to the day and evening skies.

We can't see God, but we can see his handiwork in these things, and I believe that by exploring them we can know him in deeper ways and discover spiritual parallels to our own lives.

While God is never far from his people, one must seek him to truly find him.

God said to the prophet Jeremiah, *"You will seek me and find me when you seek me with all your heart"* **(Jeremiah 29:13)**. This truth applies to all people, not just Jeremiah. One can travel to the outermost regions of the earth or be surrounded by the most intense beauty of creation and still completely miss the presence of the Creator. One must yield his or her heart and pursue him to have an encounter, and in doing so, will find that he or she is the object of pursuit.

And it is in the wilderness where one often encounters God. Elijah in the cave. John the Baptist in the wild. Jesus in the desert. Caves, wilderness, deserts—places where the silence speaks and where strength for the journey is found.

I hope this short writing may open your eyes to things once unseen or perhaps forgotten as the years have forged on through hardship, mounting responsibility, and busyness that can take its toll on vision, imagination, and dreams. I hope that the eyes of your heart may be opened to see deep things.

"I Am Who I Am..."

Consuming Fire

Chapter One

Campfires. I'm convinced they're a gift from heaven, a fingerprint of God. I can sit around them for hours at a time, whether alone or with a group. They crackle, they hiss, they pop. Sometimes they rage. They are relaxing and tranquilizing, and simultaneously wild and soul stirring. They provide heat and light on cool nights. They burn away unwanted debris and garbage. They are *alive,* constantly drawing my attention, and the gaze of anyone else nearby, to the bright flame that tramples the darkness.

After our first full day in Ontario, we spent the evening sitting around a large fire pit near the bank of the Montreal River. During our teaching time, I asked the group the question "Do you like campfires?" I remember the look on the face of one young adventurer as soon as he heard the question. His face lit up like a fire itself, eyes widened, and a smile spread across his face. "Yes!" he declared. I saw other similar expressions. I went on to ask them why, and their responses mirrored the ones listed above. There is something universal and transcendent about these bright, hot wonders.

And the best part of all is that the Bible—that old book that for some is full of dust; for others misinterpreted and haunting; for others life-changing and full of power, truth, and life—has much to say about fire.

> Therefore, since we are receiving a kingdom that cannot be shaken, let us be thankful, and so worship God acceptably with reverence and awe, for our "God is a *consuming fire.*" **Hebrews 12:28–29**

Much could be said about these verses in Hebrews. We could talk about the importance of a grateful, thankful heart and how we have so much to be appreciative of, regardless of life's circumstances. We could talk about worshipping God the right way: with all our heart, soul, mind, and strength in a way that makes us small and him very big—worship that is fueled by reverence, holy fear, and awe that comes from understanding who and what he is. And what is he? Hebrews tells us that he is a *consuming fire.*

A consuming fire. I wonder how many people see God this way. The Israelites saw him this way when looking up Mount Sinai, where his glory and power hovered over the top of the mountain. As they gazed into the fire, the gloom, and the raging storm, they begged not to hear the voice of God anymore, for it was too overwhelming:

> When the people saw the thunder and lightning and heard the trumpet and saw the mountain in smoke, they trembled with fear.

> They stayed at a distance and said to Moses, "Speak to us yourself and we will listen. But do not have God speak to us or we will die." **Exodus 20:18–19**

> The sight was so terrifying that Moses said, "I am trembling with fear." **Hebrews 12:21**

While preparing this message, I had to ask myself if God was a consuming fire in my life. Did I hold him in great reverence and holy fear, allowing him to light up my life? Or was he a distant figure whose voice I could not hear and whose presence I could not sense? I had to ask myself if I was consumed by other things.

Before going on, let's get a little familiar with Hebrews, a book written mainly to magnify the deity and supremacy of Christ. The audience was professing Christians living in Rome who were tempted to turn back to old ways (the Law) because they were being persecuted for their faith. Rome was in a time of upheaval, and Christians were a target because they were wrongly accused of bringing harm to the city.

I say "professing Christians" since not all of the readers of this letter were actual Christians. Some merely claimed to be but in reality had not truly turned away from old ways to embrace Christ as Lord over their lives. That is to say, God was not a "consuming fire" to them—not much different than many today who claim to be Christians but who are actually far from God.

Fire captivated me as a child. Many cold winter nights found me sitting in front of the fireplace for as long as possible before having to go to bed. It was a warm, safe place where nothing else in life seemed to bother me. Sitting Indian style in my pajamas, I was awed and comforted by the flames, wanting to be nowhere else.

Fire continues to woo me as an adult. During a recent summer, I served at the stables of a camp in northeast Wisconsin. One night, I rode horseback with a group of others deep into the neighboring Nicolet National Forest, where we spent most of the night around a fire.

Late in the evening, after everyone went to sleep, I kept the fire burning as the stars grew brighter and the sounds of the night came to life. I reclined on one of those fancy lawn chairs that have a leg rest, and nestled close to the flames. The temperature dropped quickly that night—not to the point of freezing, but enough to cause a chill.

After adding plenty of logs to the blaze, all was well. I gazed into the heavens, where the stars steadily increased in brightness. I daydreamed of the past, present, and future, with anticipation for what was to come. I was thankful for the experience of riding horses, for being in the outdoors, for the people I was with, and for all God had done in my life. I was in awe of my Creator—the vastness of the skies and stars, the heat of the flames, the wonder of all that surrounded me. Slowly but surely, comforted and consumed by all this, I began to drift off into sleep.

It wasn't long after, however, that I woke, shivering. In my sleep, I had shifted in my chair and was no longer facing the warmth of the fire. The fire itself had shrunk and was in need of more logs. The majority of the wood was softwood, which burns quickly. Discontented, I looked around in the dark, pestered by thoughts of bears and coyotes, the latter of which could be heard howling in the distance every now and then. I knew I had to get up and get more wood and maybe even retire to my tent. The stars no longer grabbed my attention. The peace I had enjoyed earlier seemed to dissipate.

In all this lies a great parallel to the spiritual life: *One must stay close to the fire in order to stay warm, and the fire also needs tending*. In other words, the closer we stay to God, the more we are consumed by him. The more we are consumed by him, the more peace and direction we experience, the more fiery and life giving our faith is, and the more people we influence. And all this takes some effort on our part.

We do not need a wild transformation story to experience this. We just need to draw near.

Seems obvious enough.

Yet there are those things in life that can so easily distract us and lure us away from the fire that brings warmth and comfort. These distractions can propel us toward other types of fire that are not so kind—fires that burn and leave scars.

You know what I'm referring to. Perhaps it makes you wince with discouragement and regret. Busyness, an overbooked calendar, a demanding iPad with all the applications that make you always available and connected, even when you shouldn't be. Anxiety and worry over what the future will hold, how the bills are going to be paid, the lives and well-being of your family and loved ones. Longings and desires. Trying to fit in and be accepted, approved, admired. Relational conflicts with parents, spouses, friends, co-workers. Wounds from divorce, death, loss, sexual promiscuity, broken dreams. Envy, pride, lust, addictions. Lies of an enemy who doesn't sleep, who seeks to destroy—a dark and malicious enemy of whom many are ignorant, to their demise.

The list is endless.

All these things can consume us and pull us away from the true source of warmth, light, direction, and transcendent peace.

For one to walk in the Way, in the countercultural footsteps of Jesus, with a faith that radiates the all-consuming fire of God, one must have the right weapons to fight with. The following are seven such weapons:

Taking steps of faith and obedience.

There is a one-time step of repenting of our

sins and surrendering our lives to God for salvation that goes far beyond mere intellectual belief or acknowledgement of his existence. This list of seven is useless to those who have not yet released the reigns of their lives to God by embracing Jesus's death and resurrection.

Beyond that, there are basic steps of obedience that reflect a person's willingness to grow and please God, to mature in his or her faith: becoming baptized (following cognitive repentance, non-infantile), seeking and offering forgiveness, learning to live out the Bible, serving, sharing one's faith, loving and discipling others, and sacrificing one's time for others. They are not commands intended to snuff out life, but rather to *give* life, and should be considered more of an overflow of one's devotion than a to-do list.

Basic steps—they are the key to a strong foundation. Without them, we stand on shifting sand and will not stand for long.

> We know that we have come to know him if we obey his commands. **1 John 2:3**

Spending time with God.

Just as a man and woman cannot deepen their relationship without spending quality, uninterrupted time together, one cannot stay in a vibrant, life-giving relationship with God without time spent in his presence. It comes down to the spiritual disciplines: prayer, scripture, fasting, service, solitude, and fellowship, among others.

Gordon MacDonald, in his book *A Resilient Life,* said the following of the disciplined life:

> And then, when I could appreciate them, I began to meet saints. People of faith—usually much older—who deserved the phrase used in the Bible about such people, "the world was not worthy of them." *In terms of discipline, their conditioning was the spiritual kind:* extended times of prayer, reflection, Scripture study, sacrificial service, and even suffering that was absent of complaining. I met people who gladly accepted the discipline of poverty, severe living conditions, submission to systems (and people) that were unjust and oppressive. But in spite of it all, their souls seemed to shine, and every word they spoke, every action they took, seemed to make a difference. In their presence I felt lifted toward God, and I felt a gentle persuasion to climb higher myself. (p. 153)

These saints of whom Gordon MacDonald spoke knew the value of the spiritual disciplines. They tasted the sweetness that comes from saying no to themselves and drinking deeply of the fulfilling waters of heaven that flow through us when we draw near to God.

> Come near to God and he will come near to you. **James 4:8a**

And when we spend time with God, we ought to worship him as well, as the writer of Hebrews states. He is worthy to receive it, regardless of our feelings or the season of life we are in. In worshipping him, we are lifted to brighter, higher places.

Understanding that there are seasons.

Not every day is going to be a spiritual explosion. Walking by faith will bring both sunshine and clouds, deep joy and pain, but the darkness and tears will always pass. We must hold on, wait, and press forward with hope, making the most of the day at hand. There is always much to take hold of, always work to be done, and always opportunities to bless.

We should also be mindful of the fact that it is often in the midst of difficult or mundane seasons that God is actively cultivating our faith. This can be a difficult truth to embrace, though this understanding can help ease the passage through such times.

> There is a time for everything, and a season for every activity under heaven. **Ecclesiastes 3:1**

Practicing a repentant lifestyle.

Repentance is a one-time act that paves the way to salvation. *Repent* simply means "to turn, to change direction." It is also a recurring act closely linked with confession and part of the foundation on which one builds his or her faith. While we are not to hang onto our past sin and let it hinder us, we can't deny ownership of it, either. Confess to God, and to others if necessary, and get back on the horse. No sin of ours is too great for God to forgive, and we all stumble from time to time. If we can grasp the power of God's forgiveness and grace, repentance and confession will flow more naturally.

> Produce fruit in keeping with repentance. **Luke 3:8a**

> He who conceals his sins does not prosper, but whoever confesses and renounces them finds mercy. **Proverbs 28:13**

Choosing friends wisely.

Relationships can either build up or tear down. Spending time with God-fearing people who are moving forward in faith and life will nurture our own faith and add joy to our days.

We ought to pay attention to the lives of those we surround ourselves with. Perfection is not an option, but character and heart is, and it is important to remember that it is easier to get pulled down into a pit than it is to get lifted out of one.

> He who walks with the wise grows wise, but a companion of fools suffers harm. **Proverbs 13:20**

Keeping eyes fixed on the big picture.

There is something great at work in our world. It's called the building of the Kingdom of God. It is advancing all around us, oftentimes unseen to our human eyes, and beyond just Sunday mornings. God is calling people back to him, and we can be a part of that work—that thrilling, challenging work.

I recall a well-known pastor who made the comment, "If I were starting my ministry again, I would seek to remember that, despite all its failures, the church is God's tool for reaching a lost world." And according to Jesus's words in **Mathew 16:18**, the church cannot die, not in America or anyplace else. We will face frustration, pain, and disillusionment along the way, though if we remind ourselves that church is not about us but about reaching and serving others and nurturing those who have found their way back to God, the journey will hold greater satisfaction and adventure.

> For the Son of Man came to seek and to save what was lost. **Luke 19:10**

Maintaining an awareness that we are in a battle.

In *The Lord of the Rings,* the evil Sauron is always on the move, trying to destroy Aragorn and all who stand for good, driven by fear of what they can do. The battle for Middle Earth is constant, the enemy cunning, and the stakes high.

So it is today for those who choose to follow God. There is an evil that wants to destroy us, render us useless, and lure us to compromise and passivity versus standing up for what is right and true with integrity and influence.

You know of whom I speak. For some reason God allows him to meddle in the earth's affairs, yet it's important to realize that the devil is not on the same level as God, as we see in the beginning of the book of Job. Evil is confounded by light, even ruled by it.

> For our struggle is not against flesh and blood, but against the rulers, against the authorities, against the powers of this dark world and against the spiritual forces of evil in the heavenly realms. **Ephesians 6:12**

> Be self-controlled and alert. Your enemy the devil prowls around like a roaring lion looking for someone to devour. **1 Peter 5:8**

The best things in life do not come without effort, and so it is with a good campfire. It takes work to gather the right kind of wood and maintain the flame. The more you cut and build, the more proficient and confident you become, and the whole process becomes more enjoyable and rewarding. You will also be ready to build a fire that could save your life during a storm or when you find yourself off the beaten path.

The same principle applies to relationships, including our relationship with God. To experience his fire and have our lives consumed, refined, sanctified, and empowered by it, we must be willing to do our part.

More words of fire…

Now Moses was tending the flock of Jethro his father-in-law, the priest of Midian, and he led the flock to the far side of the desert and came to Horeb, the mountain of God. There the angel of the Lord appeared to him in *flames of fire* from within a bush. Moses saw that though the bush was on fire it did not burn up. So Moses thought, "I will go over and see this strange sight—why the bush does not burn up." **Exodus 3:1–3**

By day the Lord went ahead of them in a pillar of cloud to guide them on their way and by night in a *pillar of fire* to give them light, so that they could travel by day or night. **Exodus 13:21**

To the Israelites the glory of the Lord looked like a *consuming fire* on top of the mountain. **Exodus 24:17**

For the Lord your God is a *consuming fire,* a jealous God. **Deuteronomy 4:24**

But be assured today that the Lord your God is the one who goes across ahead of you like a *devouring fire.* **Deuteronomy 9:3a**

Fire goes before him and *consumes* his foes on every side. **Psalm 97:3**

The sinners in Zion are terrified; trembling grips the godless: "Who of us can dwell with the *consuming fire*? Who of us can dwell with everlasting burning?" **Isaiah 33:14**

Above the expanse over their heads was what looked like a throne of sapphire, and high above on the throne was a figure like that of a man. I saw that from what appeared to be his waist up he looked like glowing metal, *as if full of fire,* and that from there down *he looked like fire;* and brilliant light surrounded him. **Ezekiel 1:26–27**

As I looked, thrones were set in place, and the Ancient of Days took his seat. … His throne was *flaming with fire,* and its wheels were all ablaze. A river of *fire* was flowing, coming out from before him. **Daniel 7:9–10a**

Suddenly a sound like the blowing of a violent wind came from heaven and filled the whole house where they were sitting. They saw what seemed to be *tongues of fire* that separated and came to rest on each of them. **Acts 2:2–3**

Do not put out the Spirit's *fire*… **1 Thessalonians 5:19**

God is just: He will pay back trouble to those who trouble you and give relief to you are troubled, and to us as well. This will happen when the Lord Jesus is revealed from heaven in *blazing fire* with his powerful angels. **2 Thessalonians 1:6–7**

God is a consuming fire. Our lives consumed by him make us a flame to others. His fire gives us life, healing, refining, and direction.

River of Life

Chapter Two

It was a windy, gray, drizzly evening as we sat in the small boathouse for our teaching time. It was a building full of nostalgia, a building that gave a person that warm, peaceful feeling inside. Made of old, sturdy timber, it was perched above the rocky shoreline, supported by large wooden beams that acted like legs under a table. There were also plenty of windows that allowed the eyes to absorb the beauty of the surrounding landscape.

Outside, we could hear the wind howling through the river gorge and the waves lapping against the rocks. The boats were creaking as they rubbed up against the floating dock. About a half mile west, we could see Mount Sinai through the mist—a huge wall of rock standing hundreds of feet above the water.

The river itself was immensely deep near the lodge due to the dam downriver. The dam was built decades ago, and it created a reservoir that, in some spots, caused the depth to exceed two hundred feet. The water was extremely dark, tinted with a copper hue from the tannin of maple trees that ran down the steep banks of the old forest that dominated the land. Far upriver, to the east, the river narrowed a abounded with rapids and waterfalls. Just miles in the other direction, where the sun would set, it finished its course by emptying into the cool waters of Lake Superior—the greatest of the Great Lakes.

Rivers. Wild creatures they are. Always moving, always flowing. All empty into the sea, sharing a common destiny. Yet the sea never fills. They produce wonderful sounds, ranging from trickles to roars. They are fed by outside sources: streams, smaller rivers, and falling rain. Unsuspecting logs and other objects often get stuck in their oxbows or bends. The water gets deeper and the current grows stronger the farther out you go.

There is something surreal about them. Whether a gentle stream or raging white waters, rivers, like fire, capture the soul in some mysterious way and enliven the imagination. As Mark Twain once said about the Mississippi, "It is like a wonderful book with a new story to tell everyday."

Long ago, God called a prophet named Ezekiel to go preach to his people, the Jews, who were living in captivity in a faraway land called Babylon. Within a vision that God gave Ezekiel, there was a powerful river that far exceeded the mightiness of the Mississippi. It was the river of life:

> The man brought me back to the entrance of the temple, and I saw water coming out from under the threshold of the temple toward the east (for the temple faced east). The water was coming down from under the south side of the temple, south of the altar. He then brought me out through the north gate and led me around the outside to the outer gate facing east, and the water was flowing from the south side.
>
> As the man went eastward with a measuring line in his hand, he measured off a thousand cubits and then *led me* through water that was *ankle-deep*. He measured off another thousand cubits and *led me* through water that was *knee-deep*. He measured off another thousand and *led me* through water that was *up to the waist*. He measured off another thousand, *but now it was a river that I could not cross*, because the water had risen and was deep enough to swim in – *a river that no one could cross*. He asked me, "Son of man, do you see this?"
>
> Then he led me back to the bank of the river. **Ezekiel 47:1–6**

Some scholars believe this river to be the *millennial river*—that is, a river that will be present in the future after the second coming of Christ. A more widely held interpretation is that this river is not just a thing of the future but is also symbolic of God's presence in the lives of his people. Jesus's words in the book of John seem to legitimize this belief:

> Whoever believes in me, as the Scripture has said, streams of living water will flow from within him. **John 7:38**

While the amount of interpretation and application that can be drawn from this passage in Ezekiel is limited, I believe it contains great spiritual parallels to our own lives.

Note that the man took Ezekiel *by the hand* and *led him* farther out into *deeper waters*—waters so deep that no one could cross them. I believe this parallels the fact that life and faith get deeper as we take hold of God's hand, which leads us to step out into deeper waters, to take risks and chances for eternal purposes, where all we can do is trust him with our unseen futures. In doing so, in taking hold of that great hand as a little child would, we are led to places in life that, though not always "safe," are deep, wide, and full of life.

A woman named Emily Matthews wrote a short poem called *Life's Rewards* that flows well with this principle:

Unless we take a chance or two
in order to begin,
There's nothing we can hope to gain,
no prize that we can win.
We must accept uncertainty,
must set our doubts aside,
Be brave enough to risk a loss,
or setback to our pride.
We should not be afraid of change,
or be afraid to dare –

If we just take a chance,
life holds rewards beyond compare.

If we step out and take chances and risks, especially for the sake of others, then life yields great rewards.

Yet we all know this doesn't come easy. There are always *obstacles to progress,* and they intensify as we take steps forward. And the biggest obstacle is usually ourselves. We are sometimes hindered by fear, pride, insecurity, disillusionment, depression, shame, and guilt. Hurts and wounds from our past can stir these negative feelings, almost to the point where they blind us and reduce the visibility of our dreams, sometimes rendering us incapacitated.

These wounds and negative responses to faith's challenges have no lasting power over the river of life, however. We always have a choice to reach out to the light, step into the water, and let the river wash and heal us—daily. Grace and forgiveness can always overcome.

It is true that most of these wounds never heal completely. Long after the final defeat of his enemies, Frodo, at the end of *The Lord of the Rings,* rubs his chest due to the pain caused by a wound he received on the way to Mordor. Frodo's situation mirrors real life—wounds never completely go away, though freedom from their effects increases if we stay in the river. Healing on the road takes place as we continue to move forward, not waiting to have it all together before enjoying the life and doing the work God has given us—living today while looking forward to that place called heaven, where no more pain or tears await.

> He will wipe every tear from their eyes. There will be no more death or mourning or crying or pain, for the old order of things has passed away. **Revelation 21:4**

While we don't know when that day will be, there are things we can do now—practical steps of obedience and fears to face and risks to take—that will take us deeper into life. The following are time-tested steps to follow when venturing into the river:

Surrendering

Beyond the initial moment of surrendering your life to God, there are also daily surrenders that keep faith alive and vibrant. Paying bills and taxes, submitting to and respecting an imperfect husband, loving and honoring an imperfect wife, dressing appropriately, being mindful of the words we use, respecting authority—all these things affect our faith.

Choosing to please God with every decision allows us to flow. Release to increase.

Sharing our faith

Hope is meant to be given away. We may not always feel like sharing, but there are times when God calls us to open our mouths, with gentleness and respect, regardless of our giftings and preferences.

> Always be prepared to give an answer to everyone who asks you to give the reason for the hope that you have. **1 Peter 3:15b**

Ending an unhealthy relationship

...and preparing for a healthy one. Whether friendship or romantic, relationships can affect our lives more than just about anything else. Lose the baggage.

Seeking help

We can't do life alone. I recall hearing a young girl in a camp chapel share how she was struggling with something and called home to speak with one of her leaders and ask for prayer. She instinctively knew she needed help and counsel from those more mature than her (though keep in mind that age doesn't always equal maturity). That takes courage.

I believe many youth, and especially adults, would do well to follow her example.

Doing something adventurous you've always wanted to do

Ride a horse, go skydiving, swim across a lake, drive across the country, run or walk through the woods, enter a race, ____________________ (you fill in this line). And as you're doing this, thank God for the joy and the opportunity.

Going to bed

God doesn't need us to do his work—he just lets us join in. We are all useless when burnt out and disillusioned. Sometimes we need to rest. Maybe it's time for a good fiction story or even a sabbatical—at the very least, a good night's sleep. Then get back in the race.

Additionally, if you're not one who takes the Sabbath seriously, now is a good time to start. Work hard for six days, and slow down for one. We are not too busy. It's biblical and good for us and all those around us.

> But the seventh day is a Sabbath to the Lord your God. On it you shall not do any work... **Exodus 20:10a**

> Then he said to them, "The Sabbath was made for man, not man for the Sabbath." **Mark 2:27**

Engaging your parents or children

Parents need honest encouragement and respect. Sons and daughters need the time, heart, and ears of their parents.

Technology has many benefits, but it has taken over too many family rooms, evening walks, and road trips. Know when to turn the cell phones and internet off, and do this often.

Serving your church, community, and world

Join a Bible study, youth group, or ministry and ask, "How can I help?" Go on a mission trip, or support someone who does. Sponsor a child.

Support a local nonprofit organization. Volunteer at a nursing home. Lend a helping hand to your neighbor. The list of ways to engage your world is endless.

> And do not forget to do good and to share with others, for with such sacrifices God is pleased. **Hebrews 13:16**

Challenging a friend in his or her lifestyle

A person who truly cares for another will sometimes have to get in his or her way. If we have built a bridge of friendship into someone's life, we have a responsibility to cross over into that person's land with heavy artillery. Grace and love don't nullify confrontation.

Telling and showing someone that you love them

We all enjoy that feeling of receiving genuine love and being listened to. Go and give it away to someone else. Love is action. Listen.

> Love is... **1 Corinthians 13:4**

As we step into deeper waters and apply the steps given in the previous section, something happens: we become refreshing, just like the river. Our lives splash others with life and hope.

This truth is displayed in the rest of Ezekiel's vision of the river:

> When I arrived there, I saw a great number of trees on each side of the river. He

> said to me, "This water flows toward the eastern region and goes down into the Arabah, where it enters the [Dead] Sea. When it empties into the Sea, *the water there becomes fresh.* Swarms of living creatures will live wherever the river flows. There will be large numbers of fish, because this water flows there and makes the salt water fresh; so *where the river flows everything will live.* Fishermen will stand along the shore; from En Gedi to En Eglaim there will be places for spreading nets. *The fish will be of many kinds* – like the fish of the Great Sea. *But the swamps and marshes will not become fresh;* they will be left for salt. Fruit trees of all kinds will grow on both banks of the river. Their leaves will not wither, nor will their fruit fail. *Every month they will bear, because the water from the sanctuary flows to them. Their fruit will serve for food and their leaves for healing."*
> **Ezekiel 47:7–12**

"The water there becomes fresh … so where the river flows everything will live": Where the river flows, everything becomes fresh and alive. This is powerful imagery, considering the immense salt content of the Dead Sea that the river enters and makes fresh.

"The fish will be of many kinds": Where the river flows, all kinds of fish will be caught. Many will find life. Consider Jesus's words to his disciples that they will become fishers of men.

"But the swamps and marshes will not become fresh": If the river brings life, then those not in its

current will rot and dry up like the logs in the oxbows and river bends.

"Every month [the fruit trees] will bear, because the water from the sanctuary flows to them. Their fruit will serve for food and their leaves for healing": All that is in the river's flow will grow and give life.

This final truth ought to be tattooed onto our foreheads so that every time we look in the mirror, we are reminded of God's love and the simple truth that when we stay near to him and chase after him, holding his hand and stepping into deeper waters, we become life for others.

It's not about us. God's river is flowing with life, and we can bring others into it.

> But thanks be to God, who always leads us in triumphal procession in Christ and through us spreads everywhere the fragrance of the knowledge of him. For we are to God the aroma of Christ among those who are being saved and those who are perishing. To the one we are the smell of death; to the other, *the fragrance of life.* **2 Corinthians 2:14–16a**

The fragrance of life. We can help others find life—strangers and those we love, those who are lost and weary, those who are hurting. What a gift. What a blessing. What a privilege. What a mission. Our sins and failures often try to blur this reality, though there is a river always before us—a river that is calling us to step in, offering refreshment, cleansing, and purpose.

> "A river ... has so many things to say that it is hard to know what it says to each of us."
>
> --*Norman Maclean,* A River Runs Through It

Maclean, in his widely read memoir, was mesmerized by the waters of the Big Blackfoot River in Montana, where he and his reckless brother and preacher father often found themselves diligently fly fishing for trout. They fished so much that the river became a part of them (or them a part of it). The water carried more than just fish, however. It spoke of memories of loved ones now departed, of life and death, pain and sorrow. It also spoke of something he just couldn't quite get a handle on. In a nonthreatening way, he was haunted by the river.

Like Maclean and his family, rivers seem to move us all. They get inside us with their motions and sounds. They soothe us. Slow us down. Stir us. And then they speak. Yet the river is just a messenger, and the words we hear do not come from the river itself, but from its Maker. And the voice says, *"Come, ride with me; go and tell others. Love, as I first loved you."*

"Go," says the river—run hard on earth, live the life of faith with reckless abandon, and in doing so, find the life that is truly life. Choose God, and one day, enjoy the thrill of bursting through the pearly gates of splendor when your time is up, taking hold of the eternal adventure with the great I AM.

Choose life. Get in the water.

Words from the river…

A *river* watering the garden flowed from Eden… **Genesis 2:10a**

Now the Jordan is at flood stage all during harvest. Yet as soon as the priests who carried the ark reached the Jordan and *their feet touched the water's edge,* the water from upstream stopped flowing. **Joshua 3:15–16a**

Blessed is the man who does not walk in the counsel of the wicked … But his delight is in the law of the Lord, and on his law he meditates day and night. He is like a tree planted by *streams of water,* which yields its fruit in season and whose leaf does not wither. Whatever he does prospers. **Psalm 1:1–3**

You give them drink from your *river of delights.* **Psalm 36:8b**

There is a river whose streams make glad the city of God, the holy place where the Most High dwells. **Psalm 46:4**

If only you had paid attention to my

commands, your *peace would have been like a river*… **Isaiah 48:18a**

But blessed is the man who trusts in the Lord, whose confidence is in him. He will be like a tree *planted by the water that sends out its roots by the stream*. It does not fear when heat comes; its leaves are always green. It has no worries in a year of drought and never fails to bear fruit. **Jeremiah 17:7–8**

But let justice roll on *like a river*, righteousness *like a never-failing stream!* **Amos 5:24**

On that day *living water* will flow out from Jerusalem, half to the eastern sea and half to the western sea, in summer and in winter. **Zechariah 14:8**

Jesus answered [the Samaritan woman], "If you knew the gift of God and who it is that asks you for a drink, you would have asked him and he would have given you *living water*." **John 4:10**

But *whoever drinks the water I give him will never thirst*. Indeed, the water I give him will become in him a spring of water welling up to eternal life. **John 4:14**

On the last and greatest day of the Feast, Jesus stood and said in a loud voice, "If anyone is thirsty, let him come to me and drink. Whoever believes in me, as the Scripture has said, streams of *living water will flow from within him*." **John 7:37–38**

> Then the angel showed me the *river of the water of life,* as clear as crystal, flowing from the throne of God and of the Lamb down the middle of the great street of the city. On each side of the river stood the tree of life, bearing twelve crops of fruit, yielding its fruit every month. And the leaves of the tree are for the healing of the nations. No longer will there be any curse. **Revelation 22:1–3a**

God is always leading us into deeper waters, where life and faith intensify. Step out and go. Take chances and face fears. Stay in the current—we all need others in order to stay fresh and life-giving to others.

Wild Winds

Chapter Three

The third day of our Canadian adventure found us in a large pontoon boat, motoring twenty-five miles upriver to a section of the river that narrowed considerably. Our plan was to hike up a series of pristine waterfalls and find individual quiet places along the way where we would each spend several hours alone in solitude, prayer, and meditation.

My spot turned out to be alongside the waterfall of a narrow river that fed into the Montreal. I made myself a small fire on the rock and settled in, though the rushing noise of the waterfall was so constant and dominant that I eventually had to walk upstream to find a quieter spot. Once there, the silence touched me, as did the gentle brush of the wind on my face.

At the end of the three hours, with evening setting in, we descended down blueberry-laden paths (eating our fill along the way) and returned to our entry point, where we immediately built a campfire on a large rock cliff next to the river. Directly downriver, and demanding attention, was an immensely large full moon, bright and beautiful as could be, rising slowly up from the edge of the world. In the background, the steady and unchanging sound of the rushing water could again be heard.

This sound of rushing water brought me back to a time earlier that summer when I led horseback rides through the forest. I can vividly remember riding on my horse through a trail with walls of tall red pines on each side, hearing the wind so clearly high in the tree tops. It was like a great *rushing* sound, mostly unseen, and it came and went randomly. Each time it arrested me. I sometimes wondered if my horse noticed it, too. There was just something about it—something mysterious—all around me, but I was unable to grasp it with my hands or see it with my eyes.

Wind. Another fingerprint of God that, like fire and rivers, holds great parallels to the spiritual life.

We've all probably heard it said that though we cannot see the wind, we can see its effects. Unpredictable, wild, *free*. Meteorologists can predict weather patterns, though as we all know, their inaccuracy proves our inability to get a handle on them. At times the wind is soft and soothing, brushing our faces while carrying our thoughts to far-off places. It produces distinct sounds, like those of leaves stirring. It blows away dust and dirt. It refreshes. Other times it is biting, frigid, almost cruel. It produces powerful storms by converging air from the north and south. It spreads fire.

Wind propels turbines that create clean power. It also fills sails of boats, empowering them to move through the water. Sometimes it tests sailors by appearing absent, occasionally revealing its location by creating ripples on the water called puffs, which they pursue in order to gain forward momentum and direction.

Like the wind that blows over the oceans, through the trees, down river valleys, and through our hair, there is a spiritual wind that blows upon this earth and gives power and direction to those who run with it. Perhaps you've heard of him before—his name is the Holy Spirit.

> The wind blows wherever it pleases. You hear its sound, but you cannot tell where it comes from or where it is going. So it is with everyone born of the Spirit. **John 3:8**

Wind. Spirit. This verse, spoken by Jesus to Nicodemus, weaves these words together to paint a picture of the mysterious way in which God works to bring people to salvation and infuse them with new life. Nicodemus needed to be shown how a person can be "born again."

It is interesting to note that the Greek translation of "wind" used here is *pneuma,* which can also be translated as "spirit." The Hebrew (Old Testament) word for wind, *ruah,* can also be translated as "wind" or "spirit."

In light of this, it seems there may be more to the wind that blows all around us than some may realize. To say that the Holy Spirit *is* the wind may be a stretch, though the Bible reveals a close link between the two. Consider the following verse:

> In the beginning God created the heavens and the earth. Now the earth was formless and empty, darkness was over the surface of the deep, and the Spirit of God was hovering over the waters. **Genesis 1:1–2**

Imagine: the invisible Spirit of God hovering and moving over the waters like a powerful wind, causing a stir in the great deep that would roar like a mighty hurricane. Other times, he may have been still, residing over calm, gentle waters, eagerly anticipating the dawn of man.

Some people may find it difficult to envision this scene. Similarly, it may be too much for some to grasp the idea that God can be everywhere all the time, as well as inside us. When I ponder this, I like to take a deep breath of air and think of how the Holy Spirit is like the air, the wind, in that it is everywhere. One can go anywhere and air, whether still or moving, is there, ready to breathe. Air is always hovering over the earth and in the earth, as it did in the beginning. This is comforting to me—that God can be and truly is everywhere.

Wind: unpredictable, always near but never revealing its origin or where it will blow next. Capable of bringing both relief and destruction. Untamed. Unconstrained. *Wild.*

God: unpredictable, always there but never revealing where he will show up or what he will do next. Capable of bringing both relief and destruction. Untamed. Unconstrained. *Wild.*

Perhaps you have a hard time with the frequent description of God as wild, or maybe you never considered or heard him described this way. I recall a Bible study years ago when we explored the idea of God being wild. The initial response from some was pure indignation. Depending on what comes to people's minds when they think of wild, I can understand this and even appreciate the reverence fueling the unrest.

The definition of wild proposed here is not one of being needlessly reckless; undisciplined; out of control; immersed in drugs, alcohol, and sex (like so many of the ancient "gods"); or any other view that resembles such things. That type of wild is actually chasing after the wind that leads to bondage and imprisonment, controlled by something that never satisfies but always burns and leaves one empty and unsatisfied in the end.

The American Heritage Dictionary (2nd College Edition) defines wild as: "occurring, growing, or living in a natural state; not cultivated, domesticated, or *tamed*" .

This definition, when attributed to God, is proven in life—how God works in ways that, to us, are beyond understanding. Global and national events. Situations in our own lives—

some wonderful, some painful—that come unexpectedly and offer little or no explanation

"The wind blows where it pleases…"

A wild, untamed God.

In C. S. Lewis's *Chronicles of Narnia,* there is a scene that captures this essence through the character Aslan, the hero of the story whose character is analogous to Christ:

> But amid all these rejoicings Aslan himself quietly slipped away. And when the Kings and Queens noticed that he wasn't there they said nothing about it. For Mr. Beaver had warned them, "He'll be coming and going," he had said. "One day you'll see him and another you won't. He doesn't like being tied down—and of course he has other countries to attend to. It's quite all right. He'll often drop in. Only you mustn't press him. He's *wild,* you know. Not like a *tame* lion." (*The Lion, the Witch and the Wardrobe,* p. 182. emphasis mine)

Unpredictable, untamed, unchained, not controlled or inhibited by external forces—Scripture points to a God that fits all these categories.

It is also important to remember that the "wild" acts of God are never without purpose. The Bible states that he works out all things for the good of those who love him (**Romans 8:28**). It also reveals a God who allows, or even creates, seemingly undesirable things to happen so that his glory and our joy are accomplished.

> As [Jesus] went along, he saw a man blind from birth. His disciples asked him, "Rabbi, who sinned, this man or his parents, that he was born blind?"
>
> "Neither this man nor his parents sinned," said Jesus, *"but this happened so that the work of God might be displayed in his life."* **John 9:1–3**

This passage in John can be difficult to embrace, especially for those who are currently going through trials. Nonetheless, we ought not to be too quick to judge or determine what God intends through various occurrences. His ways, which are always for our good, are beyond tracing out.

> As the heavens are higher than the earth, so are my ways higher than your ways and my thoughts than your thoughts. **Isaiah 55:9**

> Oh, the depth of the riches of the wisdom and knowledge of God! How unsearchable his judgments, and his paths beyond tracing out! **Romans 11:33**

God is free and wild like the wind, which he controls, and the more we accept this instead of trying to figure everything out, the greater peace and freedom we can enjoy.

"The wind blows where it pleases..."

And we are made in God's image—to be wild and free inside. Eve's deception and Adam's fall of long ago has resulted in many challenges for us. There is no denying this. Yet the rise of Christ is stronger than the fall of man.

To walk in this same power, however—to run with the wind and be free in our souls to live the fullest possible life, here on earth and in eternity—there is a cost. Freedom comes with a choice.

Freedom. In the movie *Braveheart,* William Wallace shouts out the word with passion amidst excruciating pain just moments before his imminent death.

Freedom. The Apostle Paul says in his letter to the Galatians, "It is for freedom that Christ has set us free" (**Galatians 5:1a**). *Freedom*. God offers it to everyone under the sun and is ready to carry it to all who turn to him, to all who choose to run with the wind instead of against it.

Yet despite this freedom and power that is available to those who desire to follow God wholeheartedly, perfection is not an option. We all fall short of perfect obedience.

In starting the teaching upon that rock ledge near the river, I asked each person to think of an admirable person of strong faith and character that they know and to share one trait about that person they appreciate. Patient, kind, understanding, joyful, positive, compassionate, challenging, bold, focused, disciplined, strong, gentle, and a good listener were among the responses.

I then went on to illustrate how these people who exemplify character and shine light on us—these people who seem to run hard with the wind, fueled by the power of God working inside them—all have their own struggles and face difficult choices. The battle doesn't end upon reaching a certain age or position.

Yet those who possess years of experience in the Christian battlefield, coupled with a willing heart that is submissive to the life-giving commands of God, have something younger people do not: they have learned many secrets of the race and have acquired a deeper understanding of the freedom they possess through the Spirit of God. Though they are not immune to the devil's arrows of discouragement and temptation, they are steadfast, even as the winds of life blow around them.

Ultimately, the greatest secret is Christ, though as we explored in previous chapters, the secrets of the race also include the disciplines that teach and allow us to live by faith. There is no complex spiritual equation for this. Trust, love, follow, learn, listen, obey, serve, repent, enjoy, go, and do.

And the more we walk by the Spirit, the more we are supernaturally transformed and the more power we have to overcome. Our desires will then become aligned with God's desires.

Inside-out change.

> This day I call heaven and earth as witnesses against you that I have set before you life and death, blessings and curses. *Now choose life,* so that you and your children may live and that you may love the Lord your God, listen to his voice, and hold fast to him. For the Lord is your life, and he will give you many years in the land he swore to give to your fathers, Abraham, Isaac and Jacob. **Deuteronomy 30:19–20**

There is a time for everything, as we know from the book of Ecclesiastes. There is a time to run with the wind, as well as a time to sit and let it flow over us and comfort us, just as it did to me that day in Canada while sitting beside the river.

There was a time recently when I recall being comforted by the wind. I was sitting in the snow and leaning against the back of my fallen horse. It was a cold winter afternoon, just hours after a bullet took the breath of life from him and ended his suffering caused by a broken leg that could not be treated. I felt so downcast inside, until I heard a sudden rush of wind travel through the trees above and break the deafening silence. The sound brought back memories of riding together through the forest and its snow-laden trails, where the flakes landed softly on our faces, creating a wonderland all around us. I recalled how I would often put my hands under the saddle blanket to keep them warm. A few times, on really cold days, I rode him bareback to take in the added heat of his body that was normally blocked by the saddle. While leaning against him that day, with the awareness setting in that our rides through all the seasons were over, I could feel the heat from his still body penetrating my jacket and warming my body. It was then that the tears began to flow. He comforted me, even in death.

The sound of the wind that day reminded me—in a way I cannot explain with words—that I was not alone. And when tempted to ask why, I was comforted not with an answer, but with the presence of the One who made that horse, the One who is aware of every sparrow that falls to the ground (**Mathew 10:29**).

The Psalmist in the Bible wrote that the winds are God's messengers, just as the flames of fire are his servants. It seems the wind that day was a messenger of comfort, pointing my thoughts heavenward.

Comfort. The Bible tells us that one of the roles of the Spirit is to comfort us, and there are those times in life when we need nothing else but to be comforted. Things happen (or don't happen) that tempt us to ask why. Sometimes we cause them, and other times they are independent of anything we did. And oftentimes, there seems to be no immediate explanation. Good and bad come to all, as the Teacher says in the book of Ecclesiastes—times of pain, confusion, sorrow, and fatigue that cannot be remedied by anything other than cries to God, stillness, the passing of time, and the gentle brush of the Spirit, which washes over our souls and reminds us that a mightier hand than our own is in control.

At the end of his book *Search for Significance,* Robert S. McGee offers words that are fitting for the unpredictable journey of faith:

> The Father is busy in our lives even when we are unaware of His activities. He wants us to find freedom in this life. He is determined that we have a chance for this freedom. Although we will never experience absolute freedom this side of heaven, if we are willing to cooperate with His plan, we can experience much more than we could ever imagine.
>
> This will be a process. It will occur only as we are willing to go to a deeper level in our relationship with Him. There will be struggles and many failures along the way. However, the Father does not get tired of being there to bring us to victory. The only question is, are we willing to go with Him?

Go, choose life, and be free like the wind.

Words carried by the wind...

But God remembered Noah and all the wild animals and the livestock that were with him in the ark, and *he sent a wind* over the earth, and the waters receded. **Genesis 8:1**

Now *a wind went out from the Lord* and drove quail in from the sea. **Numbers 11:31a**

He *makes winds his messengers,* flames of fire his servants. **Psalm 104:4**

Who has gone up to heaven and come down? Who has *gathered up the wind* in the hollow of his hands? **Proverbs 30:4a**

No man has *power over the wind* to contain it; so no one has power over the day of his death. **Ecclesiastes 8:8a**

As you do not know the *path of the wind,* or how the body is formed in a mother's womb, so you cannot understand the work of God, the Maker of all things. **Ecclesiastes 11:5**

In my wrath *I will unleash a violent wind,* and in my anger hailstones and torrents of rain will fall with destructive fury. **Ezekiel 13:13b**

He who forms the mountains, *creates the wind,* and reveals his thoughts to man... **Amos 4:13a**

[Jesus] got up, *rebuked the wind* and said to the waves, "Quiet! Be still!" Then the wind died down and it was completely calm. He said to his disciples, "Why are you so afraid? Do you still have no faith?" They were terrified and asked each other, "Who is this? *Even the wind and the waves obey him!"* **Mark 4:39–41**

Jesus answered, "I tell you the truth, no one can enter the kingdom of God unless he is born of water and the Spirit. Flesh gives birth to flesh, but the Spirit gives birth to spirit. You should not be surprised at my saying, 'You must be born again.' *The wind blows wherever it pleases.* You hear its sound, but you cannot tell where it comes from or where it is going. So it is with everyone born of the Spirit." **John 3:5–8**

When the day of Pentecost came, they were all together in one place. *Suddenly a sound like the blowing of a violent wind* came from heaven and filled the whole house where they were sitting. **Acts 2:1–2**

After this I saw four angels standing at the four corners of the earth, *holding back the four winds* of the earth to prevent any wind from blowing on the land or on the sea or on any tree. **Revelation 7:1**

We who are sealed with the Holy Spirit have the power to overcome, to run with the wind. We will sometimes stumble, though if we reach out for our

Father, he will restore us. Freedom comes with responsibility and choices. Like the wind, God is everywhere and works in ways often beyond our understanding.

Storms and Rainbows

Chapter Four

Thunderstorms. Most of us would admit that there is something wonderful about them, something that grips us no matter how many times we've experienced them. They are powerful and unstoppable, dominantly moving over the landscape with nothing to impede their destination. Unpredictable, wild, fearsome. They deliver sounds of ground-shaking, crackling thunder that makes our hearts jump, especially when it wakes us late in the night. They make us gasp by hurling bolts of lightning toward the ground that illuminate the entire sky and make us say "whoa!" as our eyes grow large. Sometimes they are soothing, providing great rains that bring a relaxing presence upon the mind and body. Other times, they deliver a light rain that produces tapping sounds on the roof and carries us into reflection and deep sleep.

Storms and rain showers shaped me as a child. I can remember being thrilled as a young boy when thunderstorms would roll through the sky above our house in central Wisconsin. The distant thunder and encroaching power moved me. Many nights I drifted into other realms while hearing the sounds they produced, and during bad storms, our mother would try as best she could to hurry us into the basement (especially if tornados were on the loose), though I'd remain upstairs or outside as long as I could.

This past summer I was awakened late one night by a great crack of thunder that may have been the loudest I ever heard. I shot up from my pillow, listening to the sound of the wind blowing forcefully through the trees and the rumbling thunder. I could stand it no longer. I slid out of bed and walked out to the porch, where I was met by an immensely dark, black sky—dark until streaks of lightning flashed above, lighting up everything in view. The wind began to blow so violently that I wondered if a tornado was approaching, and the trees were being tossed around like buoys on a lake, while leaves and debris from the forest swirled in the air above. A few times I was tempted to retreat into the safety of the house, but I just couldn't. I was captivated. Admittedly, prior to going to bed I had felt spiritually dry, but while standing under that storm, I found myself praying aloud to the God of heaven and earth, shouting out prayers for the safety of the kids at the nearby summer camp, along with various other requests that were on my heart, while thanking him for the display of his power.

The next morning I enjoyed a cup of coffee on the porch, reveling in the fresh smells and cooler temperatures that were left in the aftermath of the storm. And during breakfast at the camp shortly after, the first question out of everyone's mouth was, "Did you hear that crack of thunder?"

Storms continue to move me as an adult, though now I can stay outside as long as I want to watch these wonders. And I understand that there are different kinds of storms that we all must pass through—*storms of life*.

Our Canadian adventure group was still upriver the following night, and again we were gathered around a campfire well after dark. This time it was near the small retreat cabin that we slept in the previous night, with the river flowing just a stone's throw away. The topic this night: storms and rainbows.

To begin our teaching time, I immediately posed the question, "Do you like thunderstorms?" The response was as I suspected: "Yes!" The voices came from all around. And the answers to the "why?" question mirrored what I detailed above: thunderstorms are powerful, inspiring, soothing, thrilling. Armed with small flashlights, we took turns reading different passages in the Bible that have something to say about these fingerprints of God that we call storms:

> And these are but the outer fringe of his works; how faint the whisper we hear of him! Who then can understand the thunder of his power? **Job 26:14**

> He fills his hands with lightning and

commands it to strike its mark. His thunder announces the coming storm; even the cattle make known its approach. **Job 36:32–33**

The clouds poured down water, the skies resounded with thunder; your arrows flashed back and forth. Your thunder was heard in the whirlwind, your lightning lit up the world; the earth trembled and quaked. **Psalm 77:17–18**

After this I looked, and there before me was a door standing open in heaven. And the voice I had first heard speaking to me like a trumpet said, "Come up here, and I will show you what must take place after this." At once I was in the Spirit, and there before me was a throne in heaven with someone sitting on it. And the one who sat there had the appearance of jasper and carnelian. A rainbow, resembling an emerald, encircled the throne. Surrounding the throne were twenty-four other thrones, and seated on them were twenty-four elders. They were dressed in white and had crowns of gold on their heads. From the throne came flashes of lightning, rumblings and peals of thunder. **Revelation 4:1–5a**

I watched as the Lamb opened the first of the seven seals. Then I heard one of the four living creatures say in a voice like thunder, "Come!" **Revelation 6:1**

Then the angel took the censer, filled it with fire from the altar, and hurled it on the earth; and there came peals of thunder,

> rumblings, flashes of lightning and an earthquake. **Revelation 8:5**
>
> Then God's temple in heaven was opened, and within his temple was seen the ark of his covenant. And there came flashes of lightning, rumblings, peals of thunder, an earthquake and a great hailstorm. **Revelation 11:19**
>
> And I heard a sound from heaven like the roar of rushing waters and like a loud peal of thunder. **Revelation 14:2a**
>
> Then there came flashes of lightning, rumblings, peals of thunder and a severe earthquake. **Revelation 16:18**
>
> Then I heard what sounded like a great multitude, like the roar of rushing waters and like loud peals of thunder, shouting: "Hallelujah! For our Lord God Almighty reigns." **Revelation 19:6**

These verses paint a wonderful and fearful picture. And yet there is more. There is something that comes after the storm...

Among the responses to the question of why we like thunderstorms were those things that are left in the wake: the beauty, calm, and freshness.

As a young boy, I remember the magical feeling in the air after a storm passed one late afternoon. I came up from the basement and walked outside, where all was fresh and alive. Colors were accentuated; the leaves and grass boasted a deep, brilliant green and patches of the sky were so blue that they seemed surreal. A light mist lingered in the air that created tiny sparkles due to the rays of sunlight that had now burst through the clearing sky. The air was cooler and soft to the touch, and there was a sweet smell beyond description that filled the nostrils. Adding to the scene was a full, vibrant rainbow that was likely drawing the attention of both children and adults throughout the region.

Amidst all the wonder and greatness of storms, it is undeniable that there are different kinds of storms that we face—*storms of life.* We have all gone through difficult times and know of others who have experienced them or are currently are caught in one. Just as some thunderstorms have wreaked havoc on the lands they passed through, storms of life have had devastating effects on us and others, clipping our wings so that we cannot fly high and making it hard to see the beauty and purpose that surrounds us. They may have made us angry and desensitized, leaving us to wonder how on earth such a loving, kind, and forgiving God could allow such things to happen if he really cares and is in control.

Yet some of us have had experiences that, though seemingly hopeless at the time, have ushered in good things with their departure. Hopefully, we've seen some rainbows after life's storms have passed.

Many encouraging stories exist of storms of life and the peace that has followed:

It Is Well With My Soul. Perhaps you have heard this popular hymn, and maybe you even know the story behind it:

> Tragedy was associated with the writing of the words of this famous gospel hymn and followed closely the composing of the music. H.G. Spafford wrote the poem in the mid-Atlantic over the exact spot where his four children had drowned a few days before. His wife and children were sailing to France on the "Ville du Havre," one of the largest ships afloat. It was reamed by an English iron sailing vessel and sank to the bottom of the ocean within two hours, killing 226 people. Mrs. Spafford lived, but the four children were lost. Just weeks before this tragic drowning, Spafford had lost everything he owned in the great Chicago fire. And now, if not tested enough, he lost all of his beloved children. As soon as it could be arranged he sailed to Europe to join his wife. On the way, December 1873, the Captain of his ship pointed out to him the spot where the tragedy had occurred. Here in the dark of night, with a heart heavy with grief and pain, but yet surging with faith and hope, Spafford wrote these words:

When peace like a river attendeth my way,
When sorrow like sea-billows roll,
Whatever my lot, Thou hast taught me to say,
It is well, it is well with my soul!
(from *Stories of the Christian Hymns*
by Helen Salem Rizk)

Mr. Spafford's loss was nothing we would wish upon anyone, but after passing through immense pain and grief, he was restored to a place where he could again see light. As a result, lyrics were produced that would go on to bring comfort to many burdened souls for years to come.

* * *

I recall a trip several years ago to a small town in Mississippi that was devastated by Hurricane Katrina. I traveled with a local volunteer to deliver much-needed supplies. Though there for only a short time, I was able to see a variety of different churches come together and make a difference in that community—churches that normally would be at odds with each other. They used each other's buildings for supplies and logistics and all worked together to bring aid to the community. They worked hard, moving forward as one. Though some denominational differences are normal, legitimate, and warranted, there is a time to come together, and it was encouraging to see this cooperation.

* * *

While waiting for a church service to start, I was reading the bulletin and noticed an account of a man named Tony Snow. He faced a great storm:

> Perhaps you heard this past week that Tony Snow, a former advisor to President Bush, died from colon cancer at the age of fifty-three. I knew that he was ill. What I did not know was that he had a vital and vibrant relationship with Jesus Christ. Shortly before his death he wrote the following: "I don't have to know why I have cancer. All I need to know is that God is in control." Tony Snow understood and embraced the sovereignty of God. His words speak of his faith in the God who "made earth and the men and animals that are on the earth."

I remember seeing Mr. Snow on television. I admired his ability to speak firmly and tactfully in front of overzealous reporters. He carried a sense of genuineness and wit and appeared fit and healthy. I was both sad and surprised to hear of his passing. However, hearing his final words lifted my soul to see the beauty of his faith and unfaltering trust in God—faith and trust that allowed him to experience a supernatural peace in his last days.

***

There is another great example of one person

who endured a great storm and who kept his eye on his Maker throughout great peril. His name was Paul.

> I have worked harder, been put in jail more often, been whipped times without number, and faced death again and again. Five different times the Jews gave me thirty-nine lashes. Three times I was beaten with rods. Once I was stoned. Three times I was shipwrecked. Once I spent a whole night and a day adrift at sea. I have traveled many weary miles. I have faced danger from flooded rivers and from robbers. I have faced danger from my own people, the Jews, as well as from the Gentiles. I have faced danger in the cities, in the deserts, and on the stormy seas. And I have faced danger from men who claim to be Christian but are not. I have lived with weariness and pain and sleepless nights. Often I have been hungry and thirsty and have gone without food. Often I have shivered with cold, without enough clothing to keep me warm. Then, besides all this, I have the daily burden of how the churches are getting along. **2 Corinthians 11:23b–28 (NLT)**

The rainbow after Paul's storm may not be as clearly seen here as in the previous examples. After becoming a Christian, he lived a life marked by repeated persecution and was eventually martyred. However, we are told by Scripture that Paul discovered the secret of contentment and a peace that transcended understanding. He lived with the end in mind and left an example for many to follow.

While sitting around the fire, I asked the group to share a trial they had gone through in life and how it affected them. Most of them shared how they grew through the experience. After hearing their responses, I shared with them the accounts in the previous section and afterward asked how this may have affected their thinking of their own hard times. One of them passionately responded, "After hearing that, it makes me wonder how I could complain about some of these things in my life."

I believe he spoke courageously for all of us. Some of our storms may not be as devastating when compared with what others have gone through. Nonetheless, storms come to us all, and only by holding fast to God will we be able to penetrate the darkness and find rest when the wind is blowing hard all around us.

Our storms come in different forms…

Storms of identity and insecurity—they sweep in and tell us we're not good enough. They tear and claw at old wounds. They tell us we're not attractive or smart, and that in order to find contentment and approval, we need this item or that, him or her, that title or position. These storms distort our grasp on the fact that we have fullness as children of God and in being who he made us to be: beautiful, precious, and desired.

Storms of persecution—whether verbal or physical, they can shake our grip on the sovereignty of God. Though less persecuted in the West, we can face alienation, ridicule, and mistreatment from family, friends, and employers, all of which can test our allegiance to the One who calls us to carry our cross daily.

Storms of temptation—they can shake our foundations, try pulling us down to places where little light shines in, and attempt to steal our testimonies, relevancy, and productivity. They can blur our focus, make us feel unworthy, unclean, and guilty, make us question the depth of God's love and forgiveness and the work he has done in our lives. "Never underestimate the power of sin to destroy, or the power of God to heal and transform," I once heard said.

Storms of physical and emotional pain and suffering—they can make us ask "why?" and tempt us to turn away from God to other means of comfort. Disease, injury, depression, anxiety, or the death of a loved one can steal joy and hope.

Financial storms—whether self-induced or not, they can pull the carpet out from underneath, stirring fear and insecurity that, again, can lead us to doubt the providence of God and tempt us to turn to lesser things to find comfort and release instead of facing it head on.

Relational storms—they can leave us devastated and depleted, ripping away at family ties and friendships. Marital disputes, divorce, a wayward child, the betrayal of friendship, and a host of other scenarios can all leave unresolved bitterness and hurt that can fester for years, or decades, if not dealt with.

The list goes on. Yet for every storm, there is a choice on our part to *hold fast* and to look up. There is also a purpose involved, one that is often hard to see until after the clouds break up. In the story of Elijah and the cave, Elijah could not hear the voice of God until after the powerful wind, earthquake, and fire had passed. The voice of God came gently, in a whisper.

Long ago, God made a covenant with the Israelites—a people group whom he chose to use to make himself known. The covenant, which can be defined as an agreement that can be accepted or rejected but not altered, was marked with a sign to help them, and us, remember God's promise:

> And God said, "This is the sign of the covenant I am making between me and you and every living creature with you, a covenant for all generations to come: I have set my rainbow in the clouds, and it will be the sign of the covenant between me and the earth. Whenever I bring clouds over the earth and the rainbow appears in the clouds, I will

> remember my covenant between me and you and all living creatures of every kind. Never again will the waters become a flood to destroy all life. Whenever the rainbow appears in the clouds, I will see it and remember the everlasting covenant between God and all living creatures of every kind on the earth." **Genesis 9:12–16**

Storms produce growth and new colors, like those of a rainbow, if we hold fast to our God. Even if we stumble and fall, we can turn back and grab hold of the hand that is always reaching out to us.

In rough times it's important to remember God's covenant with us—his new covenant. The new covenant that comes through believing and surrendering to the One who was sent to redeem us. This covenant is unbreakable and undeniable, like the appearance of the rainbow after the storm.

And remember Jesus's words to his disciples nearing the time of his departure:

> I have told you these things, so that in me you may have peace. In this world you will have trouble. But take heart! I have overcome the world. **John 16:33**

Hold fast, and go…

Words for stormy weather...

Now choose life, so that you and your children may live and that you may love the Lord your God, listen to his voice, and hold fast to him. For the Lord is your life... **Deuteronomy 30:19b–20a**

The Lord said, "Go out and stand on the mountain in the presence of the Lord, for the Lord is about to pass by." Then a *great and powerful wind* tore the mountains apart and shattered the rocks before the Lord, *but the Lord was not in the wind*. After the wind there was an earthquake, but the Lord was not in the earthquake. After the earthquake came a fire, but the Lord was not in the fire. And after the fire came *a gentle whisper*. When Elijah heard it, he pulled his cloak over his face and went out and stood at the mouth of the cave. **1 Kings 19:11–13a**

Therefore everyone who hears these words of mine and puts them into practice is like a wise man who built his house on the rock. The rain came down, the streams rose, and the winds blew and beat against that house; yet it did not fall, because it had its foundation on the rock. But everyone who hears these words of mine and does not put them into practice is like a foolish man who built his house on sand. The rain came down, the streams rose, and the winds blew and beat against that house, and it fell with a great clash. **Mathew 7:24–27**

For the Son of Man in his day will be like the lightning, which flashes and lights up the sky from one end to the other. **Luke 17:24**

About midnight Paul and Silas were praying and singing hymns to God, and the other prisoners were listening to them. Suddenly there was such a violent earthquake that the foundations of the prison were shaken. **Acts 16:25**

The story of Paul's shipwreck, found in **Acts 27–28.**

For I am convinced that neither death nor life, neither angels nor demons, neither the present nor the future, nor any powers, neither height nor depth, nor anything else in all creation, will be able to separate us from the love of God that is in Christ Jesus our Lord. **Romans 8:38–39**

Consider it pure joy, my brothers, whenever you face trials of many kinds, because you know that the testing of your faith develops perseverance. **James 1:2–3**

Storms will come. Be ready for them. Hold fast while in them and understand that they are not without purpose, though that purpose is often beyond understanding. Remember who God is in the midst of them and what he has done for us. And know that the storms will pass…

Lights in the Sky

Chapter Five

The cosmos. So much mystery and infinity is involved in the expanse above that any explanation seems inadequate. To write of it is daunting and intimidating—no combination of words can be pulled together to fully capture what goes on up there. Science has made significant discoveries and findings, though the mystery still remains.

In 2004, Antony Flew, who for the last half of the twentieth century was recognized as one of the most prominent philosophical advocates of atheism, rescinded his long-held atheistic beliefs. Once a man whose personal reputation was inseparable from his atheism, he now publicly denied that life could have emerged from matter alone, and he eventually came to insist that the laws of nature could only have come from a divine mind.

When considering this, I wouldn't be surprised if Dr. Flew had his eyes on the expanse above while surveying the laws of nature that he believed stretched far beyond chance. I wouldn't be surprised if he considered how the sun, if it were any closer, would consume the earth in fire, and how we would freeze if it were any farther away. Or perhaps he considered the work of gravity or the beauty and splendor of certain stars with their size and life cycles.

Flew's change of mind was nothing short of a bombshell to all who knew him, and controversy surrounds his actual statements made in the last moments of his life. In April 2010, Antony Flew died, and while it's important to note that he didn't acknowledge the God of the Bible or Christianity, it is certain that he was convinced that life was more than just a "big bang."

The cosmos, and particularly the lights that decorate it, was the main theme for our final night in Canada. Like Flew, we believed creation resulted from something more than just a random explosion in outer space. For us, the big bang was the voice of the living God who spoke everything into being.

The skies from the prior night contributed to the discussion. Late in the evening, several of us were standing on the river bank in a state of awe over the view of the huge rock cliff, hundreds of feet high, on the other side of the water. The massive rock face was illuminated by the moonlight, and it radiated a soft neon-blue color that resembled a glow-in-the-dark sticker. Hours later, around 3 a.m., one of the guys rose from his sleep and went outside to use nature's restroom. As soon as he stepped outside into the cool air, he let out an unplanned "whoa!" at the sight of the stars shining so intensely. He unwittingly said this in such a loud whisper that he woke one of his friends sleeping inside. It made for a few laughs around the breakfast campfire later that morning.

After a hearty meal and some free time, we ventured outside and spent the rest of the evening around the campfire near the main lodge. Hearts were a bit tender as the end of our journey drew near, and a touch of both anticipation and melancholy lingered in the air. As the sky grew darker, an enormous full moon rose slowly up from the horizon on the other side of the river, adding contrast to the light blue sky. From our vantage point, it hung just above a seven-foot-tall driftwood cross that a few of the group members made earlier that day. The sight was breathtaking. It was as if the big, yellowish-white ball was joining us for the teaching, just as it did the night before.

Lights in the sky. Those brilliant starry nights that make your neck sore from looking up so much. Creative constellations that in days long past helped captains navigate through the seas and that still dazzle both young and old today. Individual stars that are so much brighter than the others, bursting with different colors as if excited by some great event in the heavens.

Then there are the mysterious, unpredictable northern lights, also known as aurora borealis, that catch you off guard and make you feel young inside as their neon colors dance across the late night or early morning sky. Even in the far North, where they are regularly seen, their activity, duration, and intensity are sporadic and untamed. Various theories as to their origin have been dispelled over the centuries (including being sunlight reflecting off the polar icecap), and even the currently held explanations are suspect.

Gentle, poignant sunrises that we always wish we could see more of, which act as a trumpet to announce the official beginning of a new day and the new opportunities that await. Blazing sunsets that paint the horizon fiery red, pink, and orange and allow us to reflect on all that has transpired, while reminding us that the past is behind us and a new day is coming.

Moonlit nights that illuminate the quiet forests and lakes, drawing the howls of wolves and the hearts of men.

Flashes of lightning that light up the land, causing both fear and excitement while reminding all that lives and breathes that a greater power is at work.

Lights in the sky: beautiful, intense, incomprehensible, and in some ways, beyond words.

Why did God make these lights in the sky?

> And God said, "Let there be lights in the expanse of the sky to separate the day from the night, and let them serve as signs to mark seasons and days and years, and let them be

> lights in the expanse of the sky to give light on the earth." And it was so. God made two great lights – the greater light to govern the day and the lesser light to govern the night. He also made the stars. God set them in the expanse of the sky to give light on the earth, to govern the day and the night, and to separate light from darkness. And God saw that it was good. And there was evening, and there was morning – the fourth day. **Genesis 1:14–19**

From reading this passage in Genesis, we see that there was purpose in creating these lights—to separate day from night; to serve as signs to mark the seasons, days, and years; and to give light on earth. This is good.

But was there more to this act of creation? Was there more to creating such an incredible display than simply separating day and night, providing light, and establishing periods of time?

When I posed this question to the group, they sure seemed to think so. Especially with that gigantic moon looming over us.

I agreed with them…

Perhaps as you read this, you may remember times in your life when you were blown away by these fingerprints of God. Before reading any further, stop for a moment and rekindle the memory of those times.

I remember a time sitting with an old friend on the shore of a northern lake, completely blown away by one of the largest full moons we had ever seen. It was seemingly within arm's reach, sitting gloriously in the sky before us, filling the earth with a radiant white glow. It cast that familiar but always mesmerizing white trail upon the water that stretched all the way from the edge of the lake right up to the shoreline in front of us. The stars were slightly diminished by its radiance, yet they still glimmered on all sides. Little did we know that it was drawing our unsurrendered hearts heavenward.

I remember a time admiring the stars while sitting in my small third-floor apartment in Chicago, brewing coffee long before dawn to accompany me for some writing. I sat close to the window and looked deep into the sky at those few stars that managed to overcome the city's light pollution. They spoke to me. I admire the city's skyline, though it pales in comparison to the real thing.

I remember gazing into the late night sky with a group of junior high boys that I was counseling for a week at a camp in the Northwoods. I planned a midnight torch hike and told them nothing of the details. With our adrenaline running high, the twelve of us departed from our cabin and walked by firelight through a wooded trail that ran alongside a lake, and then emerged from the woods into a wide-open field that was perfect for lying back on the grass and looking up. This is exactly what we did. It took some time for everyone to calm down, but once our eyes adjusted and allowed us to see the stars, the mood changed. It was a joy to hear the "ooohs" and "ahhhs" and voices yelling in a loud whisper, "Look at that!" as a shooting star caught their attention. What stuck out the most, however, was witnessing one of the boys, who came from a rough home and displayed a hard, closed heart all week long, open up for the first time while lying there, looking into infinity.

I have been wooed by the sky countless other times: walking through the moonlit woods, which cast shadows as well-defined as those found in the afternoon; sitting in the fishing boat with my father as a young boy and watching the sun slowly rise and dispel the morning fog or gently depart into the horizon beyond the trees in the evening; standing outside of an auditorium in northern Spain after a worship gathering of one thousand youth, my ears and heart fully attentive to the things of heaven, and looking up and seeing the stars screaming out while imagining people back in the States who would soon be looking at those same ones; unexpectedly seeing the northern lights in the horizon late at night while walking back to the house and halting at the sight of them.

David, the humble, courageous, God-fearing shepherd boy who would go on to become King of Israel, was moved to write the following words—words that would make one believe God had additional motives behind the creation of lights in the sky:

> The heavens declare the glory of God; the skies proclaim the work of his hands. Day after day they pour forth speech; night after night they display knowledge. There is no speech or language where their voice is not heard. Their voice goes out into all the earth, their words to the ends of the world. **Psalm 19:1–4**

As a shepherd, David likely spent many nights under the sky while out in the country. There were no lights to interfere and all kinds of time to just look up. I imagine he must have lain on his back more than once, just staring up in wonder while the sheep were safe and near.

Staring up in wonder. God created the expanse the way he did to reveal his glory, the wonder of his workmanship. He created it to reveal a message, one that is constantly crying out for all people to hear—a message that reaches to every part of the world. It is a message that has existed since the beginning of time:

> From the time the world was created, people have seen the earth and sky and all that God made. They can clearly see his invisible qualities—his eternal power and divine nature. So they have no excuse whatsoever for not knowing God. **Romans 1:20 (NLT)**

And what is that message? That he exists and is the "I AM," and that he desires our hearts.

"Indescribable," a song written by the well-known musician Chris Tomlin, beautifully illustrates this message:

> From the highest of heights to the depths of the sea,
> Creation's revealing Your majesty.
> From the colors of fall to the fragrance of spring,
> Every creature unique in the song that it sings,
> All exclaiming,
>
> Indescribable, uncontainable,
> You placed the stars in the sky and You know them by name.
> You are amazing God.
> All powerful, untamable,
> Awestruck we fall to our knees as we humbly proclaim,
> You are amazing God.
>
> Who has told every lightning bolt where it should go,
> Or seen heavenly storehouses laden with snow?
> Who imagined the sun and gives source to its light,
> Yet conceals it to bring us the coolness of night?
> None can fathom.

Indescribable. Uncontainable. Meditating on these lyrics can have a soothing effect on our minds, allowing us to see the wonders of God's creation while acknowledging that they are far too wonderful for us to fully grasp.

> He has made everything beautiful in its time. He has also set eternity in the hearts of men; yet they *cannot fathom what God has done* from beginning to end. **Ecclesiastes 3:11**

None can fathom... Louie Giglio, in his message also entitled "Indescribable," shares some incredible statistics regarding the universe:

- Relative stars and objects in the universe are as close to one another as three frozen peas scattered in the Georgia Dome (a large professional sports arena in Atlanta).
- The Milky Way Galaxy—that long stretch of foggy white you can sometimes see in the sky, and the home of our sun and earth—is just one galaxy amidst hundreds of billions of galaxies in the *known* universe. (Let me say that again: *hundreds of billions!*)
- To count all the stars in our Milky Way Galaxy, at one per second, it would take twenty-five hundred years.
- The size of the Milky Way, relative to the *known* universe, is equivalent to a quarter in an area the size of North America.

God is big. We are small. This is part of the message we ought to hear and see when contemplating these facts and when looking up and around. Dwelling on these facts can put our perspective in the right place, which is invaluable, since our perspective can so easily become distorted as we face all the daily distractions, challenges, and lies. We are, as Louie put it, "significantly insignificant." Though we are so small, God's love for us is so great. After all, he made earth and everything in it to sustain us so that he could have a relationship with us. What a wild thought.

Dwelling on God's bigness can soften our hearts and help us see that none of our problems are too big, especially for God. This is not to say we don't have hardships and angst. We will experience pain, sorrow, and confusion, though we ought to find comfort when we consider that he is right there in the midst of our suffering.

Dwelling on God's bigness allows our hearts and minds to take root with the knowledge that he is in control; we do not need to fear the uncertainties of all that is going on in the world. It's not for us to worry about the dates and times. It is for us to do well with the time and opportunities we've been given.

Dwelling on God's bigness can help us hold an appropriate view of sin and grace: big sin, big God, big grace. The more we fear and revere the Maker of the lights in the sky, the more we desire to obey him, for we know that his ways are life giving. The more we desire to obey him and enjoy the life that comes to us in doing so, the greater is the sin in our eyes that can suppress our hunger and thirst for him—the more it tears at our hearts. The greater the understanding of the destructive nature of sin, the greater the grasp and appreciation of his grace, forgiveness, and healing that comes when we sincerely return to him from the depths of our hearts, time and time again.

Dwelling on God's bigness by gazing upon those lights in the sky can also make us more of a light down here on earth.

> And we, who with unveiled faces all *reflect* the Lord's glory, are being transformed into his likeness with ever-increasing glory, which comes from the Lord, who is the Spirit. **2 Corinthians 3:18**

"Unveiled faces" refers to those who have turned away from old ways to embrace the message of Jesus, the new and only way whereby the veil—what we could call "spiritual blinders"—from our eyes is removed so that we can see the truth. Those who have the veil removed are no longer held captive by sin but rather are "slaves to righteousness," as the sixth chapter in the book of Romans points out.

The word "reflect" here can also be translated "contemplate" or "behold." In essence, what this is saying is that we become more like him as we spend time with him, beholding him and contemplating his glory and power. We are transformed more and more into his image, making our lives like a mirror, reflecting his glory for others to see.

And there are so many who need to see. There are people of every age and nationality staring into the morning sun or searching the night skies for answers, asking "why?" and crying out for something more without awareness of the hope and peace that is available to them.

We are transformed as we spend time in God's presence. Our minds, our hearts, our attitudes—these are all realigned when we linger with him. One way to do this is to spend some time under a starry or moonlit sky or in front of a sunrise or sunset. If you haven't done this in a while, or never have, then pack up your bike, car, or whatever mode of transportation you have, and go somewhere where you can be moved by these fingerprints of God. They're good for your soul.

Words of light and life…

And God said, "Let there be *light*," and there was light. **Genesis 1:3**

Let the *light* of your face shine upon us, O Lord. **Psalm 4:6b**

The moon marks off the seasons, and the sun knows when to go down. **Psalm 104:19**

Your word is a *lamp* to my feet and a *light* for my path. **Psalm 119:105**

Those who are wise will *shine like the brightness of the heavens,* and those who lead many to righteousness, like the stars for ever and ever. **Daniel 12:3**

You are the light of the world. A city on a hill cannot be hidden. Neither do people light a lamp and put it under a bowl. Instead they put it on its stand, and it gives light to everyone in the house. In the same way, *let your light shine before men,* that they may see your good deeds and praise your father in heaven. **Matthew 5:14–16**

Through him all things were made; without him nothing was made that has been made. In him was life, and that life was the light of men. The *light shines in the darkness,* but the darkness has not understood it. There came a man who was sent from God; his name was John. He came as a witness to testify concerning that light, so that through him all men might believe. He himself was not the light; he came only as a witness to the light. The *true light that gives light to every man* was coming into the world. **John 1:3–9**

When Jesus spoke again to the people, he said, "I am the light of the world. Whoever follows me will never walk in darkness, but will have the *light of life.*" **John 8:12**

For God, who said, "Let light shine out of darkness," made his *light* shine in our hearts to give us the light of the knowledge of the glory of God in the face of Christ. **2 Corinthians 4:6**

Do everything without complaining or arguing, so that you may become blameless and pure, children of God without fault in a crooked and depraved generation, in which you *shine like stars in the universe* as you hold out the word of life... **Philippians 2:14–16a**

And we have the word of the prophets made more certain, and you will do well to pay attention to it, as to *a light shining in a dark place,* until the day dawns and the morning star rises in your hearts. **2 Peter 1:19**

I, Jesus, have sent my angel to give you this testimony for the churches. I am the Root and the Offspring of David, and the *bright Morning Star.* **Revelation 22:16**

Sunsets, sunrises, stars, northern lights, and moonlit nights draw our hearts and minds to God, and remind us of his bigness and our smallness. His glory is revealed through the sky and by our lives that shine for others to see. Look up when life seems dark and out of control.

Departure

Open Our Hearts

"God, give me weather, all climates. Show me something..." I prayed these words prior to embarking on a sailing race that would span two days and approximately three hundred and thirty miles. I was young in the faith at the time and very hungry for pure life in any and every form.

Though the details of the race are for another time, it seems my prayers were heard, or perhaps influential, for we experienced an unforgettable journey: a beautiful sunset and sunrise; intense heat and humidity; a cool night with starry skies; a storm with deep thunder, lightning, and beating rain; and wild winds that made the waters swell. A memorable finish at dusk put a golden seal on the experience.

God opened my eyes and ears on that ride. It seems he has always had a way of doing that:

> ...the story of Elisha praying to God that his servant's eyes would be opened. God answered the request, and the servant of Elisha looked and saw the hills full of horses and chariots of fire all around Elisha. **2 Kings 6:17**

> ...the story of young Samuel, who heard someone speaking to him but didn't immediately recognize it to be the voice of God. Several times he heard this voice but thought it was his mentor. Finally, he was told to listen and respond if he heard the voice again.
>
> "Speak, for your servant is listening." **1 Samuel 3:10b**

> ...the story of the two men who were walking down the road to Emmaus with Jesus but didn't know it was him. Later in the evening, while sharing a meal, Jesus opened their eyes to recognize him. Later, they commented, "Were not our hearts burning within us while he talked with us on the road and opened the scriptures to us?" **Luke 24:32**

I believe we sometimes have to ask God to open our eyes and ears to his presence, his Word, and the life around us. Other times he has to get our attention. There are times when our hearts must be opened to things we normally wouldn't want to see: pain, suffering, injustice, and other storms of life.

Yet there are times when life can put a veil over our eyes and pull us away from the simple awe found in creation and the simultaneous responsibilities that accompany the Christian life. That veil can make us feel cold, spent, and brittle. Hardship and sorrow can cloud our sight and snuff out the childlike wonder inside. The state of our world and country can make us feel hopeless.

A recipe for this is to take a deep breath of fresh air each morning and look up and around, to yield our hearts and ask to see and hear, and to cry out and ask that vision would be restored. Ask that the beauty of life and the deeper spiritual meaning within it would be visible and change our hearts from the inside out, allowing us to grow younger inside as age and wisdom increase. Ask that the cries and smiles of an infant would move us, that fireflies would still dazzle us, that stars would make us feel small and special, and that the brokenness all around would rouse us.

Be mindful of a couple things, however. When the living God receives a sincere request to open the eyes and ears of his children, it will likely require an action step on our part. He may set us in front of a river, but we will have to step into it. Additionally, by making such a request, we may be submitting to a wild ride—an *adventure,* full of both joy and pain. Full of life.

And while the ride may take us to some unforgettable places (as well as some very difficult ones), I believe the greatest adventure is soul transformation—being changed so we can be agents of change. Knowing that our time here is temporal and only a shadow of things to come, we should consider it a thrill and a privilege to be a part of the redemptive work of God and his kingdom on this earth.

Best wishes, and may your race be full of light and life.

Carry us on, Great River

River of Life,

Sweep us away to that indescribable place
where heaven and earth softly embrace.
Carry us deeper into life and faith,
where the waters rise high above our waists.

Lead us to where we can clearly hear the voice
of the Great One who directs your course.
Open our eyes and ears to all that passes by:
the beauty, the purpose, and the widow's cry.

Teach us to always keep our end in sight,
to stay childlike inside as we press on in the fight,
to take the morning, to glean from the past,
through all these fleeting days that drift by so fast.

If we should travel too far into the coves
or get stuck in the river bends or oxbows,
and lose sight of the horizon, our place in the race,
draw us out, restore our vision, direction, and pace.

Let us be a carrier of your life and light,
let it flow through us into the darkest of night,
refreshing the lost and weary with hope and peace,
bringing joy, laughter, freedom, and release.

Splash us when discouragement strikes hard and fast,
when our souls are tired, crushed, lonely, or downcast,
and when the deceiver taunts us with our forgiven past.

Splash us when all seems so dark and grim,
when temptation and willful sins seek to win,
and passion for purity and others grows dim.

May your power overwhelm us,
your beauty move us,
your sounds revive us,
your water cleanse us,
your gentleness comfort us.

Carry us on, Great River,
into sweet fellowship and love with other voyagers of the Way,
into the light of the Bright Morning Star and a brand new day,
until we pass into the land where all tears and pain are forever wiped away.